THE
MAGIC PILL

*The Last Prescription You and Your Business
Will Ever Need*

Sandi Ballard, acc, cvacc

Ringmaster of the Shit Show!

ISBN: 9781726836586

DEDICATION

I dedicate this book to three kinds of people:

1. **The Quitters:** those of you who try something once and quit because it's hard. You bitch and complain that the system didn't work like "they" promised.
2. **The Do-ers:** those of you who DO things. You read a book, attend a seminar, listen to webinars or podcasts, and you DO the work. Follow the system. You MAKE shit happen.
3. **The Don't-ers:** those of you who hope and wish. You don't even try because no one will help you. No one will do what you want them to do.

You know which type of person you are. You're either ok with it, or you'd like to change. But do you know HOW?

Yes. I dedicate this book to those of you who are always in search of the short-cut, the quick-fix, or the way around the muck. To those of you who want the answers, the results, the prizes... and you want it now! You'd like a life of no challenges or frustrations. (Wouldn't we all?!)

I dedicate this book to all of you in search of the **MAGIC PILL**.

Cheers!

CONTENTS

"You can't have a million-dollar idea with a minimum-wage work ethic."
~ Stephen C. Hogan

PREFACE

Time stamp: 2018. The last three years have been a whirlwind! Ups and downs. Ins and outs. Shit going sideways.

Once you start writing books, people want to know when the NEXT one is coming! That's a great feeling, but it also puts a bit of pressure on you! I'm starting to understand how the well-known authors feel! Ok, maybe not completely. But I also do a great deal of my own "self-motivating" by putting in proposals to speak on a book that doesn't exist! I've now done this to myself... twice!

I won't say my motivation to write came easy at all. I wanted to grow my personal brand outside of Indiana and my mentor said, "You'll never be taken seriously until you write a book!"

My excuse: I'm not a book-reader, so how can I write one?

Thankfully, I was inspired to share my true self after reading a friend's book, "Campfire Leadership", by Rob Jackson. In my first book "From There to Here", I shared the "secret of my success". Well... more like the discovery of my "lack thereof" and the redirection toward a solid plan for the future.

My second book, "How Badly Do You Want 'IT'?" is more of a "how-to" type book. A "now that you've decided to do something about your life, here's how to make it happen". It came from years of working with clients, listening to their challenges and life stories, and also just random conversations that I overheard in public that drove me bat-shit crazy! And yes, some lessons that I have personally learned.

But this third book has been a bit more challenging. What could I possibly write about that's not already out there? What is it that people are looking for, wanting, and needing? What's next?

It was during this internal debate when I had a meeting with a prospective client. As she and I were discussing life, business, and why she felt she needed a coach, she informed me about the MANY workshops and seminars she and her husband had attended over the years. The vast number of self-help books she had bought. All the time and money that she had invested in the long list of programs and systems from some very well-known people whose marketing promised to show her the secret of their success.

"Yet," she continued, "NONE of them worked."

In that moment, the clouds parted. The angels started singing. Pixies riding on the backs of unicorns flew by throwing glitter! I now had the concept for my third book!

I smiled – more like smirked – when I asked her if she understood why none of these things had "worked". She chuckled as she uttered the words... "I want what everyone else wants!"

At some point in our lives, we've all been where she was. Even me! Frustrated. Desperate. Ready to give up. But this, my third book, will give you the BADASSNESS you seek, and most importantly... the secret on how and where to find the **MAGIC PILL!**

"It's common to feel uncertain, but at some point even NASA had to test the space shuttle."

~Sandi Ballard

"There are no short cuts to any place worth going"

~Helen Keller

CHAPTER ONE

THE SEARCH FOR THE MAGIC PILL

"What a fool does in the end, is what the wise do in the beginning."
~Proverb

Just because I'm a coach doesn't mean I'm any different than anyone else trying to achieve goals faster, easier, and without challenges. I've bought my fair share of lottery tickets. I have spent many of what came to be known as "hours I'll never get back" listening to webinars about the latest and greatest [fill in the blank]. I've searched for that something new... that idea no one had thought of yet! I wanted what everyone does... not just a NEW way, but a FASTER way. THE way. The answer to my prayers and the short-cut to SUCCESS. I wanted the **MAGIC PILL** just as much as you have, or perhaps do right now!

Remember, from the preface, my client who gave me the idea for this book? I said to her, "Do you realize that you're no different than many others out there, including myself at times? We've all searched for the easy way, the short-cut, the quick-fix... the **MAGIC PILL!**"

5

She shook her head "yes", owning up to the realization that all the time and money she and her husband had spent was wasted. Time and money that they would never get back.

Does that sound like anyone you know?! *Perhaps even YOU?!*

Like I mentioned, she's not alone in this sometimes painful, often expensive, and always unrewarding search. We've all seen the "promises"! Perhaps even attended, signed up, listened to, paid for, and bought into many of these **MAGIC PILLS**! They're everywhere! They're glitter-throwing pixies riding bareback on unicorns!

These programs offer things like

- 7 Steps to Becoming...
- 8 Tips for Getting...
- 9 Minutes until...
- 21 Ways to Make...
- And so many more!

Soooooooo many options!
Soooooooo many systems!
Soooooooo many opportunities!

Which one(s) have caught your attention? How many have you tried? Paid for? Followed? Whose conferences and seminars did you attend? Which ones worked?

Did YOU?

Well, sorry to rain on the parade of the million-dollar industry of "attend my seminar and purchase my system so YOU TOO can make 7-figures like me", but I have some breaking news.

I just don't know if you're ready to hear it.

You probably already know what I'm going to say, don't you? Wait for it.

Waaaaaaait for it...

Here's the secret.
The bottom line.
The inside scoop.
What the experts don't tell you.

But I will! I found the **MAGIC PILL**...

Are you ready? Do you think you can handle it?

OK then... turn the page!

IT'S

CALLED

WORK!

And HARD WORK at that!

The ingredients are:

- CONSISTENCY!
- FOCUS!
- PASSION!
- ACTION!
- DEDICATION!

...and MORE WORK!

The aforementioned systems, processes, and programs aren't necessarily scams (although there are some sketchy ones out there). The problem is, much like in my client's story, they are rarely successful due to a lack of commitment and action.

Commitment and action required of **_YOU!_** No one else can (or will) do the work for YOU!

Insert here that growly sound you make in the back of your throat when you don't like something you just heard (or in this case read). Perhaps add in an eye roll and think to yourself, "Why the HELL did I buy this book? Why bother even reading the rest of it?"

If that's really how you feel, turn to the last page for the ending (because I like the endings of my books!), and then give this book to someone who is more motivated than you to reach their goals! OR... you can read on and learn more. As a Quitter, you're going to learn how to diminish and reach beyond your self-limiting beliefs. As a Don't-er, you will learn what it takes and *how* to start getting things done. And as a Do-er, find out how much *more* you are capable of and how to encourage others to do the same.

First, ask yourself a few questions:
1. What's going on in my life, business, or career that made me search out a quick fix?
2. What made me pick up this book... why am I looking for a **MAGIC PILL?**
3. What is it that I think needs "fixing" in my life anyway?
4. What is missing? Or what is something I need to get rid of?

We all have shit going on. Every. Single. One of us! So, when someone asks "how are you", do you think they really want to know? Do we really want to tell them? It's a canned question with an anticipated reply of "I'm fine!" But deep down, we all have something we need to work on or a challenge we need help facing. And, whether it be a personal or professional challenge, we probably all know someone who's "been there"... but, unless we start asking and answering the "how are you" question honestly, we may never really know who's currently going through something and who already has. Make sense? Let me explain. We know the person, but... due to their perception, fear of judgement, and the shit that goes along with those, they probably haven't told anyone about their struggles.

Understanding that someone else has been through what you're going through can help ease the anxiety a little bit. It's ironic how, when you DO tell others about your struggles, many people will then come forward and say one of two things:

"It's happened to me", or

"I know someone who's going through that same thing."

The hard part is getting to that point where you feel comfortable enough to talk about what is going on... sometimes even with your best friends! But when you do, and you find out that you're not alone, it really does ease the anxiety and the fear of what other people think.

Although we then wonder... "Hmmm, can they help me fix my shit?"

Now, yes, you have people who can, and will, help you. But that within itself can be tricky and wildly disappointing at times because people often think they have the perfect solution. The solution may have worked for them, but will it really work for you? Now that you've asked for help, they want to fix you... but... have you really deciphered what is broken? Although their former challenge may be similar to yours now, they end up telling you what you *should* do, versus helping you identify a solution that works for you. Sort of like a "one-size fits all". When you're so desperate for the quick-fix, you tend to only focus on your challenges, and thus lose sight of the bigger picture – your goals and dreams.

You have to realize your goals and dreams are YOURS. So will others' advice even work for you? The challenges that go along with achieving your goals and dreams are not your husband's/wife's/significant other's. Not your friends'. And definitely NOT your relatives', neighbors', or colleagues'.

NO ONE ELSE'S BUT YOURS!

Now... they may have an idea of what you "SHOULD" do, and it's up to you to take that advice or leave it. No matter how excited they are for you, it's not their dream or passion on the line. And remember, no one will do the work for you! And believe me, no one can "fix" you...

Not even Dr. Phil.

"Effort only fully releases its reward after a person refuses to quit."

~Napolean Hill

CHAPTER TWO

DR. PHIL CAN'T FIX YOU

"You cannot fix what you will not face."
~James A. Baldwin

Admit it, you've watched the show! We all have at some point in our lives. WHY? Who knows? It's just like a train wreck and you can't bring yourself to look away! Or, perhaps, you're trying to feel better about... YOU.

The thing is, as a *business* coach, I tell my clients, "It's a lot of *life* and a little bit of business." It's not your business that gets in the way and causes challenges, frustrations, and failures. It's LIFE! It's the choices we make and how we allow others to impact our decisions. We can blame anyone and everything all we want. Or we can choose to get off our ass and DO!

So now what?

Do you call in for some help? Since you realize now it's LIFE that's the bitch, perhaps Dr. Phil *can* help? You spend hours you'll never get back watching, hoping, and waiting for something to resonate with you, but it doesn't.

WHAT'S BROKEN? Why do you think you need "fixed"? Let's dig deeper into this.

What are the top three challenges you are currently facing in your business?

Write them down here:

1. _____
2. _____
3. _____

Think about your business income. Is it where you'd like it to be or where you thought it would be by now? Are your sales goals being met? What about your marketing efforts? Is it your lack of passion or motivation? Are you still excited about what you do?

Passion and motivation are topics I discuss with all of my clients. I work with them to change the stress and frustration that keeps them up at night into excitement and passion that motivates them to jump out of bed in the morning. So, if stress and frustration keep you hitting the snooze button, what needs to change?

Many times, it's our environments that are the challenge. Our "environment" is the people and things that surround us at both work and home. Think about whether or not you feel organized – literally and/or figuratively. Is your office cluttered? Do you have a crooked picture or a light bulb burned out that you can't easily get to? Are you tripping over boxes, piles of paper, or stacks of file folders? These seem like silly things, but they are a mental distraction! They're chipping away at your mind. I walked by a crooked photo on my wall for MONTHS! And every time I would groan and say, "I'll get the step stool and fix that," but then I was onto the next thing on my list and the stool stayed in the closet. Until one day I couldn't take it any longer and I STOPPED myself. I went and got the step stool and straightened the damn photo! It was like a huge weight was lifted! Seem silly? Take a look around your office... no matter if you work at home or not! I bet there are at least five things that are driving your mind bat-shit crazy!

And now think about the people who you work with. Staff, colleagues, vendors, subcontractors. Does someone around you always start the day by complaining about their home-life or the traffic on the way into the office? Does someone just barge into your space and start talking about what *they* need without consideration of *your* schedule or what you might have been working on? Are your priorities or focus constantly being changed by others?

The problem is you don't say anything to anyone, and it gets to a point where the phone rings or you see "that person" and you cringe... or, better yet, hide! Whoever or whatever it is... it's digging at your soul!

And then the issue gets bigger as you take those stresses home! Friends and family start to cringe before asking about your day. And before you know it, you have become... "that person".

Now let's switch gears and get personal.

Write down three personal challenges here:

1. _____

2. _____

3. _____

Maybe one of the contributing factors to your business setbacks is the lack of support you receive from home. For example, if you are an entrepreneur and are surrounded by people who do not have an entrepreneurial mindset, it can be difficult. I've coached MANY people over the years and this is one area we talk about a lot. The non-entrepreneurs aren't used to not having a regular paycheck, the hard work, crazy hours, and constant focus on the business. Unfortunately, many times this person can be full of anxiety and not be as supportive as they could be. The mental aspect can be devastating if that support isn't there. Many times, those closest to you will poo-poo on your idea, work-ethic, or business decisions... mainly because they just don't understand!

And yes, the same clutter, chaos, and mind-numbing distractions happen in your personal world as well. Laundry. Groceries. The kids need help with homework. Pets. Family. Birthday parties. Yard work. The bills need paid. Calgon®, take me away! And, in the back of your mind, all you want to do is... NOTHING!

Maybe you try to block out or ignore your personal challenges. But, you have to remember: you are human. Life affects your business just as much as your business affects your life. So be aware of both and how they overlap. That's just what Dr. Phil would say... right?

But, since this is a book focusing on business, think about who might be the "Dr. Phil of Business". There are actually lots who qualify! Take John Maxwell, Brian Tracy, and Jack Canfield, for example. There are also the rock star women Mel Robbins and Sheryl Sandberg. How about Simon Sinek, Gary Vaynerchuk, or Greg Berry? There are so many amazing business people out there. You decide to look into their "well-known" offerings. You find some. OUCH! Some are pretty salty! But you need help with these challenges, so you start signing up.

How many simulcasts or perhaps live seminars have you attended? How many books have you paid for? How many hours of TED talks and webinars have you watched? How many podcasts have you listened to? What about the blogs you've read?

How many "pills" have you taken hoping for the magic to happen?

Have you done what they suggested? Did you do what helped THEM make 7-figures in one year? Have you followed *their* **process** – *their* **plan** – to SUCCEED? What I'm trying to say is that many of those people are making MILLIONS from selling their systems, books, seminars, coaching (which is usually done by one of their staff), etc., etc., etc. and the problem isn't with any of them...

It's YOU!

You, like hundreds of thousands of others, have been, and probably still are, in search of the quick-fix. The short-cut. What you think – or until now, thought – was the **MAGIC PILL**! Something they said resonated with you... and that's OK! Again, the problem wasn't and isn't THEM... shall I say it again? *It's YOU*! Your lack of...

WORK! ACTION! FOCUS!

As I mentioned earlier, life affects work and work affects life. And that includes all aspects of health and wellness. Financial, mental, and your physical health. Years ago, I personally was searching for the weight loss **MAGIC PILL**! *I mean, aren't we all?* I used to take a fat-blocker and then eat Mexican food for lunch. But the difference was that I would chuckle because, in the back of my mind, I <u>knew</u> it wasn't going to work! I wasn't following the system, but I wanted the "quick-fix"!

Think about this. If you want to get in better shape, lose weight, or get healthier in general, what do you do? Do you go get a gym membership? Perhaps hire a personal trainer? Sign up for Weight Watchers® like Oprah did? Or maybe NutriSystem® because, after all, it worked for Marie Osmond! Or, instead, do you peruse the internet in search of a workout you think looks easy or targets the specific area where you want fast results? I mean "7-minute abs" sounds good to me! Do you recall in 2016, actor and former pro wrestler, Dwayne "The Rock" Johnson created his app called "The Rock Clock"? Did you try it out? Did you think it could get you motivated? After all, the review on Mashable said: "The Rock's new motivational app may finally get you off your ass and into the gym". This app was built to "disrupt the traditional morning alarm system...". Ok, it may have interrupted your sleep, but did you get up and DO anything? Like anything else, it too can be snoozed, ignored, deleted... and BLAMED! Because, it didn't work.

Guess what you just did. By pointing at the alarm clock and saying it wasn't motivating enough, you just pointed three fingers back at yourself, didn't you? What didn't you do after signing up for any of these things?

EXACTLY! You didn't DO! You didn't follow the system, the plan... or the PROCESS!

Now, sometimes things can be modified. I do that with recipes. Sometimes it works, but more often it ABSOLUTELY DOES NOT! I've adjusted recipe ingredients many times to accommodate my gluten-free needs and even my daughter's vegetarian, turned vegan, back to clean-eating desires... sometimes to great success... and many times to dumping it straight in the trash.

If you modify the "recipe", what are you doing? Reducing the chances of success. And then, when you don't succeed, what will you do? Quit? Blame? Maybe both!

The thing is, they're all SYSTEMS that worked for someone somewhere at some point in their life. It's what they felt they "needed" to get through their challenge. What works for them may or may not work for YOU. I listened to Gary Vaynerchuk's audio book "Crushing It", and he said the same thing: "I'm giving you examples of what worked for me and others, but know that may not work for you."

Say you commit yourself to a system and follow it EXACTLY. What happens when that "quick-fix" is over? After the 7-steps, 21-ways, or 66-days are done... did you achieve the results you desired? Will you actually create the new habit to sustain your success? Or will you go back to your "old ways"?

As a coach, I need to help you see it on your own. I fan away the fog of self-doubt, negative perceptions, and lack of confidence to help you recognize your abilities and see your path more clearly.

So, you ask, "If Dr. Phil can't fix me, who do I trust? Who should I ask for advice?" ME of course! A coach or mentor is a great option! This is also where you start building your team. Your tribe. Those who will *help* you, NOT *tell* you what you should do, and most importantly, won't try to fix what ain't broken!

So, **who's on your team?**

> *"All of us, at certain moments of our lives, need to take advice and to receive help from other people."*
> *~Alexis Carrel*

CHAPTER THREE

WHERE MY "BITCHES" AT?

"Set your life on fire. Seek out those who fan your flames."

~Rumi

Have you found yours? You may not call yours "My Bitches", but rather your team, your people, your tribe... your boys or your girls. Whatever you call them, they are the ones you know you can count on for help, advice, and connections.

If you don't have these people yet... this needs to be a priority!

These people – your tribe – are who you are gathering around you to help with challenges, connections, and accountability so you can achieve your goals. They aren't going to lie to you, but aren't going to take it easy on you either. They will be open and honest with you – especially when you don't see eye-to-eye. They will let you know when you've lost your way (or your mind) and will be there to reel you in when you start chasing pixies riding bareback on unicorns who you SWEAR have the **MAGIC PILL**!

Maybe you have quite a few people in your world, but you just haven't tapped into their talents or found the right place for them yet. Someone may be a great friend, referral partner, or resource, but they are only part of your "tribe" for a specific area of your life.

Take a look at WHY, and HOW you're asking for help. Even more importantly, you need to remember that, no matter what they're helping you do (work on a new project, achieve a personal health goal, create an event, or develop an idea), it's YOUR goal. YOUR dream. *Not theirs.* They may love your idea, goal, or product/service... and they may love you! But they can only be tools in your toolbox. They are there to HELP you achieve your success. They aren't going to DO it for you!

Yes, you will have some that try to take it on as "theirs". Or they may not help at all and disappoint you. Sometimes you will need to make some hard choices and stop asking certain people for help.

You may have continually asked the same people to help with EVERYTHING and it doesn't always work out. And in some instances, they may even start "disappearing". I've fallen victim to this. I wanted everyone to help with what **I** needed or thought they **should** help with, but I didn't ask if they CAN or WILL help. Did they even want to? They may have wanted to, but perhaps the timing wasn't good. I've told people "no" and "not right now" before. Recently, I was asked to help lead a committee, however, I was maxed on my volunteering and helping others, and told her I would be available in a couple months when my previous commitments were finished. It wasn't "no". It was "not right now".

Learning to say no can be hard sometimes! How many of you have said no and felt good about it? How many of you felt awful, or perhaps did NOT say no and regretted it? Or did you AVOID saying no by just not answering? I was speaking at a conference once and, during Q&A, one of the attendees actually said that was her M.O.. Instead of saying no, she would tell the person that she would check her calendar, and then just not get back with them! WOW! WHAT? She went on to share that most of the time, the person asking never circled back.

I believe in being honest! I had someone from one of my tribes tell me no once after she had originally said yes. The thing is, she was honest and said she was overwhelmed with her own business and she needed to finish a big project she had committed to. I was a little mad at first, but I appreciated her honesty and her commitment to HER clients. MY ask for her to help me, was for MY goal, not hers. And by being honest, she earned even more of my respect!

It took me a lot of time to find my different tribes. There have been YEARS of frustration that went along with asking for help and depending upon others. I thought my best friends – my oldest friends – would help me on a moment's notice with ANYTHING I needed! I even thought they should have offered to help without me having to ask! Many times, we expect our family to do the same. I wasted a great deal of time and energy being pissed-off and frustrated with people. All because of EXPECTATIONS I created! You've probably been there as well! Setting expectations can be dangerous if you don't discuss them and just ASSUME people will help, like I have.

Ok, grab that pen again!

Write down five times you've been disappointed. Next to it, by whom. And why (if you know).

DISAPPOINTMENT	BY WHOM	WHY?
_____	_____	_____
_____	_____	_____
_____	_____	_____
_____	_____	_____
_____	_____	_____

Take time to reflect on these situations. Do you now recognize how these were YOUR expectations and not THEIR offer or agreement to help? Do you understand how expectations can cause frustration and even damage personal and professional relationships?

I was told once by someone, "If you didn't expect so much out of people, you wouldn't be so disappointed all the time." I realize that I expect a great deal out of people. But what this person was telling me (that I didn't HEAR) is that I wasn't ASKING or communicating what my expectations were. I was merely assuming people would just DO things. We all know what happens when you ASSUME something, don't we? Just in case: When you **ASSUME**, you make an **ASS** out of **U** and **ME**. And it's so true! And that's why it's so important to find your "bitches"!

Since I had always been so disappointed in people, I had adapted to the concept that so many of us do: "If I want it done right, it's easier to just do it myself". It took me years and many instances of needing help to truly understand what "building a team for success" meant. Yes, even as a coach, I didn't quite get it. (I love calling myself out!) I realize now that life is a TEAM sport!

Once I understood the concept of having a tribe, I started looking at people differently – especially the women around me. When I asked for help, I listened to their response, watched how they reacted, and evaluated how fast they stepped up, if they did at all. I'd pay attention to whether or not I had to remind, prod, or BEG. Did they agree to help just because I'm a friend or were they on board because they believed in what I was doing? I learned quickly if someone was helping with or without genuine interest.

After the first TABOO! Women's Luncheon in March of 2017, I had three people contact me afterward commenting about how great the event was. I knew at that moment that they were "my bitches" for this event! But, I didn't just ASSUME. I told them how much I appreciated their initial help with the event and that I knew there was *no way* I could continue to make this event grow on my own. I ASKED if they would be interested in forming a TABOO! committee. They had helped make the first one a success, but not in an official capacity, so this wasn't something they should take lightly! Luckily, they all said YES!! They all have different networks, skills, and talents and that's what makes a good "tribe".

I have other people who help me by sharing my weekly podcast titled "No More Excuses". This "tribe" is actually spread all over the world and has taken my podcasts with it. I have others I call upon and meet with for networking and business-focused questions. My other "bitches" are ones that I call or text when I need to vent about personal shit, knowing they aren't going to *tell* me what to do or try to *fix* me or the situation... they are there just to allow me the space to let it all out, and vice versa!

I've learned to ask certain people for help with specific areas of my life. For some aspects, I need people I can trust 1,000,000,000%. For other instances, my tribe can be a more casual group of friends or colleagues. Some people will cross over to multiple tribes, but I have allowed THEM to make that decision.

What about you? Who's in your world? Think about it.

Make a list of 5-7 people you can trust, depend on, or confide in. People who you admire and perhaps even have values that align with yours. Then, next to their name, write what you'd like them to help with. Now... ASK them!

No, seriously! Set this book down right now and contact at least one person on your list. Ask them for their help where *you* think you need them. Once you've talked with them, use the last space to document whether they said YES or NO!

PEOPLE YOU TRUST	HOW CAN THEY HELP	WILL THEY HELP
_____	_____	_____
_____	_____	_____
_____	_____	_____
_____	_____	_____
_____	_____	_____
_____	_____	_____
_____	_____	_____

How'd it go? How did that exercise make you feel? What emotions came up for you? Were you hesitant to even do this exercise or anxious about how the person would answer? How did it feel to speak with someone about a challenge in your life, an area where you need help? And yes, how did it feel to ASK for help?

I understand that asking for help can sometimes be the hardest thing to do. So you just don't! Were you afraid the person on the other end of the phone would question why you need help? Maybe even challenge you as to why you are doing what you're doing? Many people don't ask for help due to these false perceptions! "What will they think of me if I need help?" Or even worse, "What if they tell me NO??" You think you know their answer before you even pick up the phone!

(Pssst! Have you ever considered the fact that some people are grateful and even flattered that you asked them for help!?!)

Ok. So you finally brought yourself to dial the number. Did you get a "no"? Or a "not right now"? That's alright, because each no get you closer to YES! Trust me I understand! I've been in your shoes! I've had that, "why won't anyone help me" moment! It's the false perceptions causing the head trash and anxiety that are keeping you from asking. Hence the reason you're stuck, frustrated, and searching for the quick fix! Well, guess what! The **MAGIC PILL** here is ASKING for help!

Now, continue down the list. As I said, it's OK to get a no! And this exercise also helps you learn who and how to ask for help. If they answer no, or not right now, politely say, "I appreciate your honesty" and move onto the next person. But wait a moment. What if this time when you share your challenge, instead of you telling the person how you'd like them to help, you ask them to tell you how *they* think they can help? See if that changes their answer. Sometimes we pigeonhole people and ask them to help in an area of what we think is their expertise instead of relying on their confidence and experiences. Again, we may not know they've gone through a similar challenge until we ask!

And again, if you get a no, ask if they know someone who has faced a similar challenge and may be willing to help. It's not always the person closest to us that can, or should, help us. It may be someone that just didn't pop into our minds to ask! We've all had that moment of, "Oh yeah! I didn't even think about her/him!" And, in a sense, the person who said no actually did help!

So, have you completed your list? If not, *why not?* Are you just going to skip ahead in this book and see what's next? If there's something else that will help? Well... you're going to need to do this at some point! As scary as it may seem, and as heavy as the phone may feel, it will be a HUGE step in your personal and professional growth!

Ok, so you've gone back and now you did it. Well... what did they say?

When you were talking with your list of people, did your ask change based on their comments or reaction? That's ok, as some people may have talents, skills, or connections you didn't realize. Maybe you assumed they would want to help in a certain area because of what they do for a living, but they surprised you by wanting to help in a different aspect altogether. Heck! Maybe they even volunteered to help with more than one tribe!

Are you excited about the tribe(s) you just created? Yes, you may have gotten some questions, piqued some curiosity, and perhaps even been challenged by someone questioning your goal or purpose. But that's good! Those people might be "your people" for a different tribe because they've been honest! Now, once you get the no's, the questions, and the proverbial "I'm not sure what you're doing is such a good idea" bullshit comments out of the way, and finally get a "HELL YES", you can breathe a sigh of relief and realize... that wasn't so bad after all, was it?

Be careful to not ask too much of one person so as to not burn them out! It's also important to make sure you're not asking someone to help just because they are successful at what they do. What you are doing is different than what they do. How they got there is different than how you will get to your destination. And, just because someone has a natural ability or skill set, it may mean they just got around to *swallowing* the **MAGIC PILL** a little sooner than you!

And remember, no one, no matter how successful they are, is your **MAGIC PILL**!

"Your life is yours and yours alone. Rise up and live it."
~Terry Goodkind

CHAPTER FOUR

PERCEPTION IS NOT REALITY

"Your Perception May Not Be My Reality."
~Aporva Kala

We all have someone that we admire (or maybe even have been jealous of) because of their natural abilities or their success. We somehow acquired a perception that this person "has it easy" or "is a natural"... probably even thinking "they don't have to work that hard" at whatever it is they do.

Make a list of five people who you feel "have it easy". (Celebrity status or someone in your life.)

1. _____
2. _____
3. _____
4. _____
5. _____

Let's start with the example of professional athletes. Do you think Peyton Manning just woke up one day and was one of the best quarterbacks in the NFL? What about Michael Jordan? Flo-Jo? Tiger Woods, or even Serena Williams? Yes, maybe these people have natural athletic talent, as do so many others, but had they not worked at it, someone else would have been better! These athletes didn't take short-cuts or the easy way. But, what they did do was find and take their **MAGIC PILL**! Remember, that means WORK!, CONSISTENCY!, and FOCUS!

We associate hard work and effort with athletes, but think about all the business professionals, product creators, and visionaries in every industry... they all have what it takes to succeed! They have the passion and commitment to not just "get by", but to *excel* at what they do. They don't look for the short-cuts. While they're always striving for new, better, and more efficient ways to get the job done, they aren't cutting corners or taking the easy way out.

There's a very long list of amazingly talented people in every industry – music, art, science, business, sports. Some are very famous while others we may never hear of. Well-known examples that pop into my mind are: Mark Zuckerberg, Richard Branson, Madonna, Condoleezza Rice, or even the late, great Michael Jackson. We also have the rags to riches Oprah Winfrey and J.K. Rowling. And the list goes on! We have heard the stories of some of these people. Their struggles and frustrations. How they've had to restart, rebuild... pivot. But until we heard their story, all we saw was their SUCCESS. How they made it look easy. Until recently, it wasn't acceptable to share your challenges with people. You didn't want others to know about your failures – personal, professional, or financial.

These individuals and many more had what it takes and didn't give up! They put in the blood, sweat, and tears! To some of you, it may still appear to have been easy, but what they had was the *real* **MAGIC PILL**!

Refer back to the list you made at the beginning of the chapter and take the time to learn their story. If it's a celebrity, try to find an article or story about them. I've learned a lot about people I admire by watching documentaries or reading about them. If it's someone you know, a local success story, or maybe someone in your same industry, reach out to schedule lunch or coffee and just ask about their life and successes. People are more willing than you may think to share their story and offer advice.

Maybe that person on your list passed an industry-specific test the first time and you didn't. Perhaps he or she got through college in less time or was promoted before you. There are people everywhere that we perceive to have it easy. We somehow think they are just smarter, stronger, or more talented but, until we dig deeper, we don't see the hard work they put in.

When people found out my daughter was graduating college in three years, everyone that I talked to had comments, questions, and even surprised expressions. "How did she do it?," people would ask. Well, she worked her ASS off! The school she attended had quarters instead of semesters, which allowed her to start earlier than many of her friends who attended traditional universities. This format also allowed her to attend school year-round! She didn't come home for the summer, or any quarter for that matter. She popped in here and there for a couple of weeks at Christmas, but that was it! It was INTENSE! She took no mental break and was thousands of miles away from her high school friends, her family, and her entire support system.

So how did she survive and excel so far from her "people"? Well, she had to build a new tribe to give her the support she needed to make it through 36 straight months of school. This tribe – her "girl gang", as she called them – helped her stay FOCUSED and MOTIVATED on her goal: saving money by graduating in three years. While creating her plan, she realized she had to pay year-round for her school lodging and parking, so why come back to Indiana for the summer? Going continuously would help save a great deal of money! And that's what she did! She did not allow distractions, even though she was young, worked an off-campus job, and lived in the most year-round-greatest-weather state! (I know I, personally, would have skipped school many times to be at the beach!)

I am sure she's not the only kid that has accomplished this. I'm guessing many of you reading this know of someone similar and may have thought it appeared easy or a short-cut. My great aunt graduated high school at 16 and went on to Cornell. She was obviously brilliant, but, did she look for quick fixes? Did she "have it easy"? Hell no! Many of the upper classmen didn't feel she should be there. Many parents didn't think such a young woman, considering the era, should be in college at that age, if at all. She had to work twice as hard to PROVE that she DESERVED to be there.

Now, we've all met those people who DO take the easy way. Even I've done it once or twice. For example, I had all my credits to graduate early from high school, but then the school removed the early graduation option. So, to retaliate against the new policy, my senior year of high school was filled with easy classes! Not one challenged me. Looking back, I realize that, without challenges, I also lacked growth.

Time to grab that pen again!

Make a list of three to five times that you now realize you "took the easy way". The next step may take some thought! Why did you take that short cut and what did you hope to avoid by doing so?

SHORT CUT   **WHY?**

_____   _____

_____   _____

_____   _____

_____   _____

_____   _____

Who do you know who would always read the CliffsNotes™ instead of the whole book in school because they didn't plan well enough to read the whole thing? (*raises hand*) How many times have you googled words for a Words With Friends® game instead of accepting the lower score? What about taking supplements or pills that promise fast results instead of cutting back on certain foods, adjusting portion sizes or adding in a physical fitness routine?

So what made your list? Facing WHY we sometimes took the easy way, quick-fix, or short cut can help us identify when we're doing it again. Sometimes we just want dessert first, right?!

Think about the people we've come across who always want someone else to "do it for them".

I'm referring to the people who really won't do more than the bare minimum for themselves. Those people don't want to put in the extra effort and seem like they are perfectly fine with where they are, or so we think. (Again, our perception.) Who knows what they are really thinking?! I've come across people like this and, if you can get them to open up, many times they <u>do</u> want more. They're just afraid to admit that they need help. That they can't do it all themselves.

Now it's *their* perception of what others think of *them*! They can't ask for help if people think they have their shit together, now can they? That would be embarrassing! They believe people will think less of them for *needing* the help. They may assume they'll lose the respect of others, because after all, they are the "mentor, boss or leader", right? Trust me, I know that first-hand! In my first book, I told everyone about how I hid my need for help for years!

Yes, there will always be those who whine, bitch, and complain about how hard it is to work through challenges. I know all too well that there are those who you just can't help. My mentor told me once, "Sandi, *you can't want it more than they do.*" Sometimes you have to dig a little deeper to figure out if someone truly wants help taking a step forward or just the short cut of having someone do it for them.

Now take a moment to reassess what you thought you needed to fix or why you wanted to take the short cut to achieve a goal. Are you comfortable saying things are as good as they'll get? That "this is the best I can do, and all that I will become." When you think about the possibilities, do you tell yourself "there's always my next life"?

The bottom line is that you just gotta GET OFF YOUR ASS and DO! Nike® was sort of onto something with their tagline, "Just Do It". Don't ya think? It's their mantra. Their mission. What they live by and truly believe.

What about you? Are you ready to LIVE? Are you ready to DO? Or would you rather continue to be jealous of others who appear to have it easy?

Now that you have put some thought to your life, and gone through the activities in the first four chapters of this book, has your mindset changed? Are you still thinking about taking the easy way and searching for what you thought was the **MAGIC PILL**?

Or, are you willing to put in the WORK to make amazingly great shit happen?!?

It's a choice. As I ended my second book, "I choose SUCCESS. I choose 'IT'... how about you?"

You need to understand that your success or *lack-of*, truly, without a doubt, lies in the choices you make.

"I never dreamed about success, I worked for it."

~Estee Lauder

CHAPTER FIVE

THIS OR THAT?

"Every morning you have two choices: Continue to sleep with your dreams or wake up and chase them." ~Unknown

Choices can be hard. That's part of life and why many of you reading this book have a hard time making them. So you just... don't. *Do you*? Guess what! As the RUSH song "Freewill" goes, "Even if you choose not to decide, you still have made a choice!"

I recently had a client who came to me and said, "I want to make healthier choices". Although we did end up working on all aspects of her life, we started initially with her personal health. She liked her fast food sandwich and pop (or soda, whatever you call it!) for breakfast, yet she wanted to lose weight and feel better. If you've seen the movie "Supersize Me", you know you can't have fast food every day and expect to lose weight, let alone feel better! So, we worked on her choices. I had her adopt the "This or That" theory. I never told her she couldn't have fast food for breakfast, but we discussed the options and the pros and cons of continuing this unhealthy habit. I've used "This or That" myself for years! Instead of dessert, I'll have a glass of wine. Most people choose "AND", but what if you choose "OR"?

My client was doing great! She was also working with a nutritionist and was weighing in weekly. We would walk during our sessions instead of just sitting and talking (and eating!) and she was learning to make healthier choices.

But then... if you're following along with the theme of this book, you may guess what started to happen. The results weren't coming as fast as she wanted. She decided to go to health fair and talk with someone about Bariatric surgery. Yep. The "quick fix". The "short-cut". The "easy way"... her **MAGIC PILL**!

She called me for advice. I'm sure she could sense my disappointment, but instead of telling her what she *should* do, we talked about the pros and cons of her having the surgery. I asked her WHY... many, *many* times. Her answer was always that she didn't like how slow the weight was coming off, and she admitted that the healthier choices had been difficult.

During our next session, we reviewed her goals and discussed her expectations. Both needed to be modified. Her goals were aggressive and led to very high expectations of herself, which, in turn, didn't match with her willpower. As much as her current support system would help when she wanted it, unfortunately they also didn't step up when she truly needed it. That doesn't mean it's their fault and she should blame them... which is what she had a tendency to do. Instead, she really needed to find more inner strength, take accountability for her actions, and search for different people to be on her health & wellness tribe.

We all know what happens with any new choice... it's not a habit until it becomes part of your life. It needs to become something you want to do, or just do without thinking about "having to". Kind of like breathing!

Since that call for advice, my client and I have discussed other options in regards to her plan to achieve her goal. She has made some adjustments, including allowing herself to have a "cheat day" and NOT beat herself up about it! (The guilt you put on yourself is when the problem continues into a downward spiral, which I love to refer to as "Bon-Bon Moments".) She also has learned to be happy with herself and, going back to Chapter two, she has made major changes with her support system at home. The outcome was that she chose to keep on keeping on as-is, and *not* have the surgery. And more importantly, not regret the decision she made. You need make the decision and move on.

Again, the habits have to become part of your life, not just for a short time. That's why many fad diets (i.e. Whole30®, "intermittent fasting", NutriSystem® and Weight Watchers®) don't work. Because people tend to use them as a "quick-fix" versus adopting that plan as a lifestyle. And that's why I despise the "21-days to...", "7-Steps to...", "9-Minutes to...", and other quick fixes. Those short-term focuses can make a difference, however if you go back to your unhealthy habits, we all know what happens, don't we?

The bottom line is that you may find the **MAGIC PILL**, but you still have to swallow it! You need to do more than just understand the work that needs to be done to achieve your goals. You must DO the work!

Trust me, I LOVE tacos, queso, french fries, pizza, cheeseburgers, FOOOD! Did I mention tacos?! And that doesn't even include after-dinner treats! But

I make choices. A lot of choices. And not just with my health. Making choices, deciding if you want "This or That", is all part of life and how we learn and grow. The same applies to how we evolve as business owners, managers, and leaders!

Every single day we make choices. We get bombarded with ways to market our business, where to network, how to do more, *make* more, BE more. You may be thinking about whether or not to change jobs or how to move up in your current career path. If you have a business, should you create new products, or do you add, delete, or maybe just modify the services you offer? What's the right answer? What if it's wrong? What if it doesn't work?

What if it DOES?!

Thinking too much without action can cloud your decision-making process, and will seriously hurt your brain! Overthinking has definitely hurt mine! Haven't we all done it, though? Business is down. A client cancels... again. A customer doesn't reorder. Someone unsubscribes from your list or unfollows you (it happens to me every month!). Perhaps they choose another business over yours. You start questioning what you're doing, your pricing, the services you offer, or products you sell. You think to yourself, "Should I offer something new? Perhaps a lower price, or better options?"

I've over-thought myself right into MANY wasted hours of wonder! I've sometimes just stared out the window, or sat outside in a chair and zoned out looking at the trees. I've actually yelled at myself in the mirror to STOP thinking! There have even been a couple of times when I've laid down on the floor in the middle of my office and just cleared my head!! I suppose that was my form of "meditation" to quiet my mind! However *you* choose to **STOP** the voices and clear your mind is up to you, but it is necessary sometimes so you can then go back and think clearly about what is going on.

Do you really want or need to try something new? Do those changes make sense? And if so, how? Will they help you get back on track? Will you still be aligned with your vision, mission, and values?

Here's an exercise I do with many of my clients. If you have an idea or are contemplating changing something, what are the pros and cons? WHY do you think it needs to change? Is it just a knee-jerk reaction or is it something no one bought, liked, or gave a shit about?

Choose something you're thinking about changing and write it below.

_____

Next what are the pros and cons of this product or service:

PROS	CONS
_____	_____
_____	_____
_____	_____
_____	_____
_____	_____

Do the pros outweigh the cons or vice versa?

Keep in mind that one pro or one con could have a much higher significance than another. For example, perhaps the pros are that it is a lot of fun, easy to market, and doesn't take much time to develop, however the con is that it doesn't bring in much money. Is it worth the time and effort it takes just to make the smallest amount of revenue?

Really think about this. What does your gut tell you? Does it really need to change?

Circle one: Yes   No

IF NO: then why did this potential change make your list?

What made you think it needed to be changed or removed from your offerings? Why are you second-guessing it... or are you second-guessing yourself? If that's the case, then there's probably some underlying confidence issues. Have you had a previous failure with this or something else? Did you get negative feedback about this item? I understand how one comment can make you rethink your whole focus, let alone one item, portion, or aspect of your life. Just because someone didn't like something you said, or a product you sell, doesn't mean it's broken! And it definitely doesn't mean you have to change it... at least immediately. And frankly, we can't please 'em all, can we?! (Remember, we aren't for everyone and not everyone is for us!)

It is good practice to review what you offer. And *how* you offer it. Again, take some time, ask people, do the activities in this book before you jump at any quick decisions. Things do need to change to keep up with the times, technology, and industry demand. Those changes, however, don't have to happen overnight or after one shitty review or comment!

So, if the cons aren't outweighing the pros, then take it off the list and focus on something else.

IF YES: it does need to change, then how? Does it need to be reworked, repriced, or even deleted altogether? What can you do to make this more beneficial for your clients, and/or more profitable for you?

Once you have identified an item that needs to change, the next step is to develop a plan to implement the change. Every potential change looks different for each person. This may be a good time to call in help from a coach – like me – or someone from your tribe.

Repeat the pros and cons exercise as many times as needed to address all areas of uncertainty.

Taking the time to make choices can be difficult as well. It's easy to NOT make choices, *isn't it?* And sometimes you just *avoid* making the choice by continuing to "do". I know I preach to "JUST DO" a lot, but are you actually *doing* what you _need_ to be doing? Or are you simply going through the motions and avoiding taking the time... no... **MAKING** the time to face these sometimes very hard realities?

Chapter six of my second book, "How Badly Do You Want 'IT'?", is all about change and how painful it can be if you resist! Change is necessary, maybe a necessary evil, but it's what allows for growth! So you may choose to kick and scream and put off the changes that need to be made, but in the end, what usually happens? You realize... "Why did I wait so long?" or even, "That wasn't so bad!" Even unexpected changes can be favorable sometimes. It's something you weren't thinking about that somehow presented itself.

For example, I submitted a proposal to speak at a national conference. I was so excited to see that it was accepted that I didn't read the entire acceptance letter. Oops! Once I started getting more information and deadlines to submit my slides and worksheets for the attendees, I noticed something was different. "Hmmm, this says I'm speaking during an Ignite session vs. the Express Talks. What's the difference?" Fifteen minutes. That doesn't seem like it should be a big deal, but it wasn't anything I had done before! It's a fast-paced FIVE minute talk where the slides change automatically every 15 seconds. Only five minutes and I'm not in control! YIKES!

Ok, so I've done the 15-20 minute talks and I've facilitated countless full breakout sessions, but this just seemed so... FAST! Why was this so unnerving to me? Well, first, it means I will have to cram my 15-minute talk into FIVE minutes. Secondly, it means I DON'T HAVE CONTROL! I almost didn't go! I thought to myself, "Why bother to go for ONLY five minutes?" As I always do, I posted on social media about the talk. It turns out I didn't get the support I thought I'd get! People were saying the same thing that I had thought: why bother for five minutes? But that really wasn't what I *needed*! I was searching for someone to say, "HELL YES! DO IT!" So, what did I do? How did I decide? I did the "Pros and Cons" activity!

The pros outweighed the cons. I recognized that it was a national conference in Chicago that had more of my target market in attendance than many of the other presentations I had given to date. It was time for me to pivot. To completely step out of my comfort zone by letting go of control! It was time for me to not just grow, but to grow *forward*.

The day arrived. It was time to practice with the others. I walked into the room and saw that about 400 chairs had been set up to face the stage! Until that day, the largest crowd I had spoken to had been around 250 people. I thought I might throw up! I think I even said that during my practice session!

One woman who was in the lineup said she thought they were closing off half the room. They did NOT! We got through the practice session and it was GO-TIME! I left the room to get some water. When I walked back in, the room was damn near full... ALREADY! By the time our session began, there were over 400 people in the room! People were standing alongside the wall! I was excited, anxious... and prepared!

My hard work and practice shined throughout my full five minutes! I nailed the timing of the slides and had the whole room engaged. Afterward, some of the attendees told me they loved how interactive my talk was, even with it being only five minutes. I now understand that this specific breakout session was one in high demand! Everyone LOVES the stories, the lessons, and the format, and it showed! I left the conference with more confidence, as well as a few prospects. As a speaker, I grew and evolved!

It's a choice to tune out the Negative Nellys, the "should-ers", or the ones that got you second guessing in the first place! You can choose to listen to them or you can choose to stop all the voices and rationally think through things yourself. You can even call in "your bitches" for help now that you have a tribe!

What I'm suggesting you do is STOP searching for the quick-fixes and easy-way-outs and DO the work! It's time to start making your own decisions on how to grow, pivot, and evolve.

"It is not the strongest person who wins in life, but it is the most nimble, flexible, and adaptive person who wins in life."

~Debasish Mridha

CHAPTER SIX

IT'S EVOLUTION BABY!

"Change is inevitable. Evolution, however is optional." ~*Tony Robbins*

Things change. As humans, we adapt to change by growing and evolving. Change is inevitable. Resistance is futile™.

So, how do we evolve? Evolution is science after all, isn't it? Darwin's Theory. Evolution is about the ability to survive and develop new skill sets. It is a CHOICE. In my (always awesome) opinion, as we DO things – take action, as well as risks – we LEARN from our mistakes along the way. Which, in turn, is EVOLVING, *right?*!

And here's the thing, if you don't *learn* from your mistakes, that's when you get stuck. We all know someone who we've said, "Wow, they are just stuck in the '80's!" Why do you think they won't let go of that hairdo? Those jeans or that favorite t-shirt? **FEAR!** They live in their fuzzy-slippered comfort zone and say they are perfectly happy, but deep down they are afraid of the future! Afraid if they give up something that they once loved or reminds them of the "best time of their life", that they won't be happy. Now, I'm sure all of this runs more on the side of what a licensed therapist would get into, but I'm here to touch on just their lack of GROWTH! If you're stuck, what are you NOT doing? Making a choice! Ok, ok, yes! You're still making a choice to STAY where you are, but think about what you are depriving yourself of! The opportunity to learn and grow!

Think about how you've grown and evolved over the years. You may notice subtle changes about people as they get older, and that's because they're learning, growing, and evolving. Instead of asking your friends, colleagues, or (if you're daring) family how you've *changed*, ask them how you're *different* or how you've *grown*.

We evolve as humans as we take steps out of our comfort zones and try new things. Take the exercise in Chapter five for example. You were making choices on **if** and **how** to make changes. Many times, it's based on how you've grown and evolved. Where are you now as a person? What stage in your life are you in? What's changed? Are you single, married, have kids, or even grandkids? Have your priorities changed? And how does that affect your business or career? Things may change based on trends. If you make a food product and offer different flavors, you may decide to jump on a bandwagon or create a new, unique flavor yourself! Think about popcorn! It's not just salt and butter anymore, is it?!

I recently watched the HBO series Silicon Valley, a show about the ever-changing world of technology. During several of the episodes, they talk about "pivoting" as a company. They stayed fluid and would "pivot" as the market demanded or as a new opportunity presented itself. The important thing is, the management as well as the staff had to evolve first to allow for the company to pivot. Basically, they would offer a new product and/or service as competition became fierce or, in this case, they were losing ground to the larger company with unlimited funds! They made a choice to allow change to happen. And it was sometimes painful. As the main character in the show evolved as a leader, he allowed for the growth of the company, which, in turn, boosted the confidence of his staff... and, their company's reputation!

As a business coach, I have pivoted my focus more than once. For example, I started out with no group sessions! I only worked with people individually and held business-focused workshops. Then, through what I thought was a one-time group activity (intended to get a handful of clients to take action), I received multiple requests from the participants to create a monthly accountability group. So, what did I do? I pivoted.

As people heard about the groups, I created more. At one point, I had five – yes FIVE – monthly accountability groups in addition to all of the individual coaching clients and business building responsibilities. As each group began, I imagined that they would all follow the same agenda. However, it never ceased to amaze me that each group would somehow take on a life of its own and go in a different direction with a completely different focus than the other groups. So as much as I wanted it to be "easy" (ha-ha), with the same agendas, topics, and worksheets every week, I learned quickly it wasn't about what I wanted. Each accountability group was evolving to meet the needs of the clients in it. I had to make the CHOICE to evolve my own way of thinking for the success of the groups and the individuals. Once again, I pivoted as the industry demanded.

By pivoting, my group accountability sessions gained so much traction, it caught the attention of another coach who was a doctoral student and needed to do some research for his final dissertation. He was writing his thesis on the benefits of group coaching and how it was helping entrepreneurs. Group coaching wasn't well-known at the time, and I was one of the few coaches who was doing it successfully. He wanted to interview me and my clients about the concept, the process, and how it was helping them grow and succeed both personally and professionally. He even flew out to Indiana from Boston to meet me and conduct some of the interviews in-person!

Fast forward to 2018. I'm now down to ONE group. Yep, *only one*. But, my individual clients are back up! Most of my clients, who are now further along in their business, come in every three weeks for 90 minutes to two hours, versus the more traditional coaching which is one hour every other week. I'm pivoting as my clients themselves are evolving. Their businesses are growing so their needs are changing.

You may have noticed that I didn't mention workshops in my current range of services. Well, that's because the exercise from Chapter five, helped me recognize that as much as I LOVED business-focused workshops (pro) the time, effort, marketing, and cost all fell into the con category. I really enjoyed doing them! I loved the training aspect as well as helping people grow and have "Aha" moments! I also really enjoyed watching people who attended and didn't know each other at all, easily connect and sometimes even give each other referrals for business! But... each workshop took SO MUCH time, effort, and money to market.

As you grow, learn, and make choices to pivot, it's beneficial to assess what you offer, how you offer it, and WHY! How is it aligning with your goals and bigger vision of who you want to become?

At the beginning of 2018, I did this for myself. I wrote down all of the buckets that I focus on and what each brought to the table, so-to-speak. How does each area help me achieve my goals.

This is going to be your exercise for this chapter! So once again, grab some paper and a pen or get over to that white board!

Step 1: Get a stack of Post-it® notes. Write the name of each category of products/services your company offers on individual Post-it® notes and then stick them onto a white board or a larger piece of paper.

Step 2: Underneath the main category on each Post-it® note, write down the purpose or goal of offering this product/service.

Step 3: Choose one Post-it® note. Draw an arrow from that category's Post-it® to another category that is affected by it. Does that second category also have an effect back on the first? If so, draw a line to/from it as well. Do this for all the notes.

You may also find you have a Post-it® note that has no lines/arrows draw to or from it. If so, go back to Chapter two and complete that exercise for that category as it may be a product/service that needs to be reworked.

Turn the page to see the results from my Post-it® note exercise.

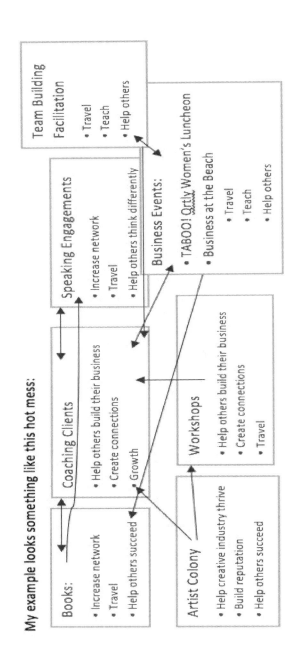

My example looks something like this hot mess:

Books:
- Increase network
- Travel
- Help others succeed

Coaching Clients
- Help others build their business
- Create connections
- Growth

Speaking Engagements
- Increase network
- Travel
- Help others think differently

Team Building Facilitation
- Travel
- Teach
- Help others

Business Events:
- TABOO! Qrtly Women's Luncheon
- Business at the Beach
- Travel
- Teach
- Help others

Artist Colony
- Help creative industry thrive
- Build reputation
- Help others succeed

Workshops
- Help others build their business
- Create connections
- Travel

Yes, I know there are many more efficient graphs I could have used, but I literally just grabbed a piece of paper and started writing things down.

This helped me identify WHY things were in my life, and how it was attached to, and aligned with my overarching goal/big vision of myself. What I realized was how they were all intertwined! The latter, to me, was the most important as it can tell you if you are focusing on things that don't connect. It's ok to do many things, just ensure that they *connect to* versus *distract from* one another.

I know people who do many things and attempt to justify how they interact by saying, "I've been told not to depend on one stream of income." Those people get frustrated with me as I question their WHY. I challenge them on how well they are doing in each of these areas. Where you focus your energy is where you'll see growth, right? So, if you're running three businesses that don't connect in some way, how efficient is that? And how productive are you? Take another look at my graph.

I'm a business coach, which is one thing, but all the services I offer create multiple streams of income. At first glance, you may think that writing books, facilitating team building events, and being a public speaker are, or could be, three separate businesses. However, as you see how the arrows connect, in the end, they all help me find clients. And so those activities, events, and even the books are part of my marketing tools. They help me build my business, which, in turn, helps others build theirs. By doing speaking engagements, I get to travel, which is one of my goals, and I usually get more clients. By getting more clients, I obviously generate more income, and, thus, get to travel!

As I continue to learn, grow, pivot, and evolve in each of these buckets, it helps me achieve my goals and live the life of my dreams. No one else's! Once you do this activity, see where you are and how your buckets align with your goals. How do they help you create excitement and passion for what you do. Remember, you need to transition the anxiety that keeps you up at night into the excitement that gets you out of bed in the morning ready to KICK ASS!!

"Evolve or Dissolve...
It's your decision."
~Larry Price

CHAPTER SEVEN

DETOUR AHEAD!

"There is no path to happiness. Happiness IS the path."
~Buddha

Pssst! Hey you!

You look lost! Come this way!

I know what you're looking for! I know the way.

You've learned a lot about, and understand what the **MAGIC PILL** is now, right? Ok good. So, let's get you back on the right path. I'll show you the way to "Happy Land"!

Yes... **HAPPY LAND!**

What the HELL is "Happy Land"? As I state in my last book, the definition of "Happy Land" is:

The place you day-dream about regularly. It's the place where you have achieved your goals and done all of the things you have ever imagined, but never believed you could. It's your "happily ever after" world.

Perhaps, even after you've read this book, and understand what the **MAGIC PILL** really is, you aren't sure that you even want to take it and get to "Happy Land"! Just like the **MAGIC PILL**, the truth is hard to swallow, isn't it? Is it because you don't think you can ever get to this magical place called "Happy Land"? That it will never become your reality?

The thing is, it CAN be reality!!! The only problem is you've always been searching for the wrong thing! You've been led down a path of false perceptions! You thought the **MAGIC PILL** was a quick-fix, a short-cut, or a much, *much* easier road with no bumps, road blocks, or wrong turns! Perhaps you may have even been led to believe that you'd never find the right path.

I've been there. Some days I feel like I'm STILL there! And that's what all these exercises are about. They are in this and my previous books because I have been through every bit of it! I'm sharing with you my process.

Let me tell you a story.

I was in Houston in early 2018 speaking at the SMPS Regional Conference (Society of Marketing Professional Services). After I was finished, I wanted to try something new, so I booked us (my Man-Candy, Tad, and I) on a horseback riding adventure. Since we currently don't ride horses and neither of us had been on one since our childhood, we decided it would probably be in our best interest to do the beginner trail. (Although not part of my nature, I actually almost booked us the half-day ride, and then I started thinking about the ability to walk the next day!) So, I chose to take the completely acceptable option of baby steps! As our new adventure began, I was handed the reigns to my horse, Dusty. He was a white-ish color and he was... DUSTY! He was a good horse for the most part, but about halfway through the ride, as I was getting bored and restless with the slower pace myself, it appeared he was as well. It was at that moment that I realized something about Dusty.

Let me preface this by saying I was the last horse in line. So as the team of horses ahead of us would stop and go, Dusty and I were like the last in line of a car wreck. I found myself constantly watching to see if the other horses up ahead had stopped or which way they were going. As it turns out, Dusty kind of knew what he was doing, however, he managed to catch me off-guard the first time he stopped to "smell the roses" while the other horses continued onward. Once Dusty decided he was ready to go again, he quickly picked up his canter! Boy, was I glad I listened to the initial instructions from the trail leader on how to "stand-up" a little if they take off jogging, as my butt could have been seriously bruised!

So, we've caught up to the team. The pace was back to a slow walk. And then... he did it AGAIN! Naturally, I started paying closer attention and that's when I picked up on the fact that he did not like mud! As we continued with the ride, I heard the other horses trudging through the muck. I watched what was happening from atop my horse. Dusty would abruptly STOP and then look around! Hmmm... he was looking for a way AROUND the mud. The muck. The BULLSHIT that he didn't want to go through to get to the "other side"! He would pause and look to the right, and then to the left. And eventually trudge through it, like the others. As he did this multiple times, I thought to myself, this is exactly what my clients do! They want to AVOID the mud. The muck. The dirty work. The crap. **The BULLSHIT!**

However, the only way to "Happy Land" is straight through the muck! Yes, through all the shit storms, frustrations, speed bumps, and whatever else comes your way! And it takes work. HARD WORK. Much like Dusty. That horse was constantly looking for a way around the "muck", but would eventually realize, with the help of my "gentle prodding" in his side, that the only way to the other side was THROUGH. There was no detour or way around this mud puddle he faced. Sometimes we do come across full-blown road blocks where a detour is necessary and available. But what happens? You find your way back with a little help or guidance, and sometimes you may even learn new and unexpected things along the way! And yep, it's what I have to do many times with my clients... gentle prodding with my "pointy shoe"!

It's interesting how an animal can learn much like we do. And how I watched this happen and made the connection. Had I not chosen to try something new, this observation would have never happened... and maybe not this chapter! I learned a lot from Dusty that day. I guess, in a sense, I evolved a little as I smiled and realized how life is like that trail ride.

During March and the beginning of the NCAA tournament, the theme of one of my weekly podcasts was PASSION. I talked about how some of the teams and individual players seem to have what it takes to get through the tough games, even double overtime! And also, as some of the underdogs beat the top seeds, how can they, and did they keep going? That month in my accountability coaching group, I brought up the podcast and the theme of "passion". I asked the members if they had the passion to get through the rough spots, the frustrations and challenges of business... the muck. One of the members of the group said, "Passion is necessary, but you have to have the commitment as well." I TOTALLY AGREED with her!

Think about it. You can be excited about doing something and want it so badly, but are you *committed* to staying on the path and doing the work it will take to achieve it? Or the opposite... do you think you're committed to a goal, yet you aren't *passionate* about it? You don't go to bed or get up in the morning EXCITED about what you have in front of you? You have to have BOTH! There is no passion without excitement, and how can you be excited about something where there is no passion?

I want you to think about what keeps you up at night. What gets you out of bed in the morning? Is it the same excitement or is it dread? And what are the choices that go along with it? What are you choosing to do? What's keeping you from being excited and passionate about something? What needs to happen to help you?

It's all choices.

If you are willing to swallow the **MAGIC PILL**, think about how much you will be able to experience! All the learning, growing, and evolving that will happen! But, it's up to you to decide because, yes, it involves change, and change can be painful if you resist it!

One of the biggest hurdles I believe people need to overcome is to realize what they've already accomplished. Acknowledge that they have kicked ass and achieved more than they give themselves credit for.

Getting to HAPPY LAND – Success – is obtainable... BY YOU! Let go of the perception that billionaires, professional athletes, or A-List actors didn't have to work for it! It's not a glittery unicorn of a myth! Although I started this book to dispel many of the "get-rich-quick" schemes out there, I learned myself that it's not the plans, programs, and processes that are the problem. The issue is the people who buy them and then not follow the system.

So, what if we all start with one simple task... acknowledging that we all have inner BADASSNESS! You just have to know where and how to find it!

"I truly believe that everything that we do and everyone that we meet is put in our path for a purpose. There are no accidents; we're all teachers - if we're willing to pay attention to the lessons we learn, trust our positive instincts and not be afraid to take risks or wait for some miracle to come knocking at our door."
~Marla Gibbs

CHAPTER EIGHT

FINISHING YOUR BADASSNESS

"There's nothing as unstoppable as a freight train full of fuck-yeah."

~Jen Sincero

We all have it. Badassness that is. What do you think? Are YOU a badass? Not sure? Trust me I ask that question to many of the groups I speak to, and I rarely get many hands raised. When I do get some hands to go up, it's usually a very shy, uncertain hand that only raises up to about ear-level. You know, just in case they need to quickly retract or perhaps act like they were just scratching their head! I love when I see that happen! Not to call anyone out, but to take the opportunity to dive into the WHY. Why are they so unsure about their badassness?

So, why do we bury it deep inside us versus letting it out to sparkle!? Is it self-doubt? Is it the fear that people will think we're bragging? Somewhere along the path of life, we have adopted this perception that being a BADASS and sharing our achievements is considered bragging. Why is that? Why are we bragging if we talk about ourselves and our successes? Maybe it's because the person listening to our successes has buried their own badassness and is jealous of yours. We tend to allow others to tell us if we are successful or not instead of owning it ourselves and letting it shine! Is it a lack of self-confidence or is it because we aren't quite sure what success really means to us? Success, as my second book referenced, is defined by YOU. No one else. Most people haven't taken the time to define what it means to themselves. And, then, yes, we don't know HOW to achieve it, which leads us to where we start chasing shiny objects. Pixies on unicorns and what we once thought was the **MAGIC PILL**.

At the time I am writing this book, there have been many days where I wonder if I'll ever achieve more. Will I sell more of this book than my previous ones? Will I get "the call" to be a keynote speaker? I wonder if I'll ever get to the top of my "Mount Everest". But how am I even measuring my success?

First, I need to figure out what success means to me. I define success as significance! Let me explain a bit more. As I help people achieve their goals, I play a role in their life, which, in turn, helps me feel "significant". To me, that means I have achieved SUCCESS! I have helped people take steps toward, and many have achieved their goals and are onto the bigger vision of themselves.

Take a moment to really reflect upon what success means to you.

Write down your definition of success:

_____

_____

Think about all that you HAVE achieved! No matter how small or insignificant it may seem. Many of you are probably like some of my clients, who say, "All in a day's work!" and sort of just move on. I like to stop those clients and say, "Hey that's a big SUCCESS!" with a long pause to allow them the opportunity to let it sink in. We'll exchange a celebratory high-five and, many times, I'll email them after our meeting just to point it out to them AGAIN! Especially for the over-achievers! It's hard to get them to relish in their achievements, even though that's what they're after. Ironic, isn't it?!

It's time for another activity! I want to get you thinking about your successes. Make a list of 3-5 things you have achieved. (Even if you or someone else doesn't think it's a big deal.)

1. _____
2. _____
3. _____
4. _____
5. _____

I've done this exercise with many groups before, including my TABOO! Women's Luncheon. After some gentle nudging, I can always get some people to finally stand up and proclaim in front of the group one of their achievements. They admitted it was something they didn't really talk about as they felt others may think they were bragging!

Some of the things the people said were:
- "I bought my first house at 23."
- "I made the IBJ's 40 Under 40 list." (Indiana Business Journal... trust me it's a big deal... a goal I never achieved.)
- "I created an all-natural skin care line from scratch."

- "I got on stage at a concert to sing with my favorite band."
- "I ran a marathon."

I mean, Hell, I didn't start running until I was 40! And I won my first 5k! I used to reduce the "bragging" by saying, "Well it was a small race and there were only a few people in my age group." THAT DOESN'T MATTER! A win's a win, baby!

You've got to talk about the successes – that fact that you HAVE achieved goals – and HOW you did it.

And how, exactly, did you achieve those goals? You swallowed the **MAGIC PILL**! You did, in fact, work for it. And it doesn't matter if your accomplishment was successfully growing a tomato plant!

Go back to the list again and take a few moments to really look at it. Bask in the feeling of accomplishment! Now smile and say out loud, "Look at what I HAVE done... I AM A BADASS!"

If you are struggling with the exercises in this chapter, go back and re-read my second book, "How Badly Do You Want 'IT'?". You will find step-by-step instructions on how to achieve the success you desire. I help you see where the blame, bullshit, and excuses have caused you to get "stuck in the 80's" and how perfection can cause you to live a life of regret! You'll learn that it's never too late to start working toward and living the life you dream of!

My goal with this book is to help you realize that you already are a BADASS, you just have to dig down to find it, and then let it out! Acknowledge your accomplishments and SHOUT them to the world! STOP perceiving that talking about your badassness and achievements is bragging. STOP assuming that each individual who appears to "have it easy" hasn't worked their ass off! And finally, STOP searching for the quick-fix, easy-way, or the shortcut, and understand that success isn't easy, but it's definitely worth it!

So, here's the deal. Read the books. Watch the TED talks and the webinars. Attend the conferences and seminars. Listen to the podcasts. Play "This or That".

Even watch Dr. Phil.

But, just remember...

Those **MAGIC PILLS** only work when <u>YOU</u> do.

It's still a choice. Your choice.

And now that I know what the **MAGIC PILL** really is, I choose to get off my ass, put in the work, and make amazing shit happen!

What do YOU choose?

"A dream doesn't become reality through magic; it takes sweat, determination, and hard work."

~Colin Powell

Made in the USA
Columbia, SC
22 November 2022

71427277R00043